What Did the Angels Say?

Lori Taetz

WHAT DID THE ANGELS SAY?
Copyright © 2025 Lori Taetz

All rights reserved. Neither this publication nor any part of this publication may be reproduced or transmitted in any form or by any means, electronic or mechanical, including photocopying, recording or any information storage and retrieval system, without permission in writing from the author.

This is a work of fiction. Names, characters, places and incidents either are the product of the author's imagination or are used fictitiously, and any resemblance to actual persons, living or dead, businesses, companies, events, or locales is entirely coincidental.

Scripture taken from the New King James Version®. Copyright © 1982 by Thomas Nelson. Used by permission. All rights reserved.

Print ISBN: 978-1-4866-2755-4
Hardcover ISBN: 978-1-4866-2757-8
eBook ISBN: 978-1-4866-2756-1

Ages 6-8
Grades 1-3

Word Alive Press
119 De Baets Street, Winnipeg, MB R2J 3R9
www.wordalivepress.ca

This book belongs to:

_____

This book is dedicated to my children
—Jericho, Malibu, Harmony, and Shiloh.

Thank you for teaching me the importance of learning the stories of Jesus and pondering them in our hearts.

Angels appeared on the first Christmas day.
Tell me the story.
What did they say?

"God has come to earth today.
You'll find Him in a bed of hay.
This Baby has come to be our King.
Glory in the highest, we will sing."

Shepherds trembled on the first Christmas day.
Tell me the story.
What did they say?

"A host of angels filled the sky.
'Glory to God!' they sang on high.
Let's go and see the tiny Boy.
He will bring us peace and joy."

The star shone bright on the first Christmas day.
Tell me the story.
What did it say?

"The heavens declare God's awesome glory!
I will shed my light on this story.
My brightness will shine from celestial skies
To mark the place where Jesus lies."

Wise men searched on the first Christmas day.
Tell me the story.
What did they say?

"We're from the East. Men call us wise.
We saw a star as we studied the skies.
Let's find this King whom the prophets foretold.
We'll bring Him incense, myrrh, and gold."

Animals watched on the first Christmas day.
Tell me the story.
What did they say?

"He is the Lamb. See how He sleeps,
Nestled in straw with the donkeys and sheep.
Our Creator born in a stall
Peacefully sleeping, Savior to all."

Joseph kneeled on the first Christmas day.
Tell me the story.
What did he say?

"Our Child has arrived, and I am so glad
That down here on earth, I can be His dad.
He's God's only Son, but I'm just a man.
Chosen by God to be part of His plan."

Mary prayed on the first Christmas day.
Tell me the story.
What did she say?

"This beautiful Baby, my only Son.
Our Gift from the Father. The chosen One!
This Child is from heaven; God's love He brings.
My heart will forever ponder these things."

When we celebrate on Christmas day
And tell the story,
what should we say?

"Sent straight from heaven, with a love so great,
Now all of God's children can celebrate!"

You've come down to earth to make all things new.
Happy birthday, dear Jesus! Happy birthday to You!

www.ingramcontent.com/pod-product-compliance
Lightning Source LLC
LaVergne TN
LVHW072102070426
835508LV00002B/237